DINOSAURS

Sara Hurst

Illustrated by Lucy Cripps

Kane Miller
A DIVISION OF EDC PUBLISHING

Dinosaurs were alive long
before there were people.

Meet them as you explore their world of
dense forests, steamy jungles and shallow seas.
See how they live and why they become extinct,
and find out how we know so much about them today.

Shine a flashlight behind the pages to reveal
what is hidden and discover a prehistoric
world filled with surprises.

Dinosaurs weren't the first animals on Earth.

Life began millions of years earlier in the seas and lakes that covered the world.

Let's take a look.

The first living things
are simple organisms.

Over time, many different kinds
of plants and animals appear, and
some move from water onto land.

Early fish

Jellyfish

Bristle worm

Soon, new types of plants cover the land and different animal groups appear.

One group is a kind of reptile. Can you guess what it is?

The dinosaurs!

As time goes on, new kinds of dinosaur appear. They quickly become the biggest, most awesome animal group on land.

Pisanosaurus

Plateosaurus

Eoraptor

Many of the earliest dinosaurs are small. *Coelophysis* is only about three feet tall and is a fierce hunter!

What else shares its world?

Splash!

This hippopotamus-like creature, called
Placerias, isn't a dinosaur but a mammal-like
reptile. It has a beak for snipping plants
to eat and tusks to defend itself.

Something is behind this cycad plant, darting away from the huge sauropod foot.

What is it?

It's *Compsognathus*.

This speedy dinosaur runs quickly on two legs. It is the size of a turkey—that's really small for a dinosaur!

Zoom!

Giraffatitan is taller than a four-story building! Its long neck reaches up, stretching to pull tough leaves from the treetops.

How does its massive neck move so easily?

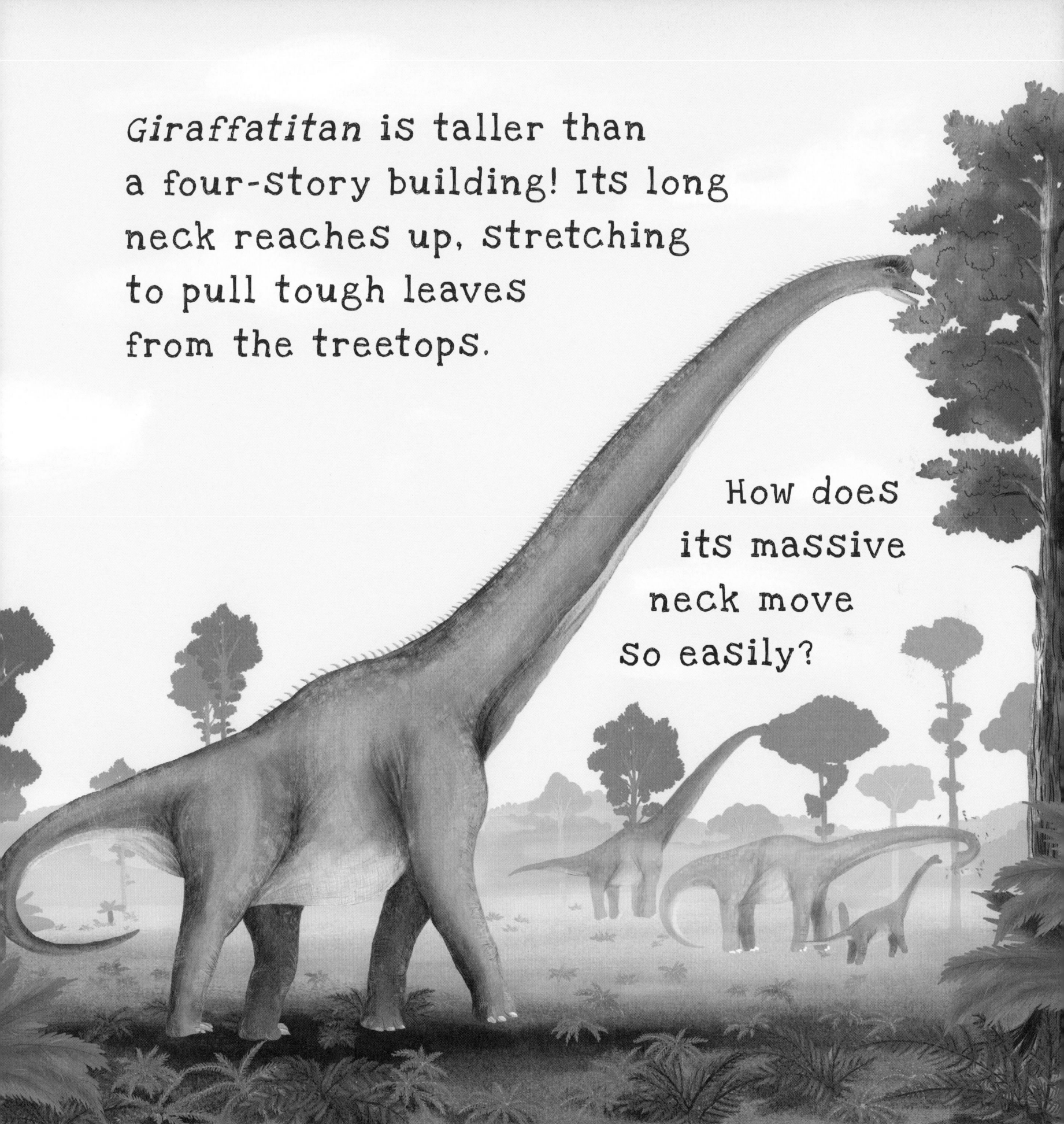

Munch!

Air Spaces

Air spaces in the heavy bones make the neck light. Its small head and brain don't weigh much either.

This *Stegosaurus* family has found a patch of tasty horsetail plants. The plates along the adult's back have turned pink to send a signal to the others.

What is in the treetop?

whoosh!

This small, furry mammal is jumping and gliding from tree to tree.

Its name is *Volaticotherium*.

Archaeopteryx
is an early kind of bird.
It has a beak with sharp
teeth and long feathers all over
its body. What does it look
like without them?

A tiny dinosaur!

Archaeopteryx is
descended from
a group of small
meat-eating dinosaurs.

Flap!

A *Maiasaura* has scooped out a deep, round nest in the sand. It stays nearby and watches over it.

How many eggs has it laid?

Five eggs!

Dinosaurs are reptiles, so they lay eggs. Dinosaur hatchlings stay in the nest and are fed by their parents.

Crack!

Parasaurolophus are feeding by the water.

One is making booming sounds through its head crest.
Can you see why?

It's a *Deinosuchus*, one
of the first crocodiles!

Parasaurolophus hoot through
their crest to warn each
other of danger.

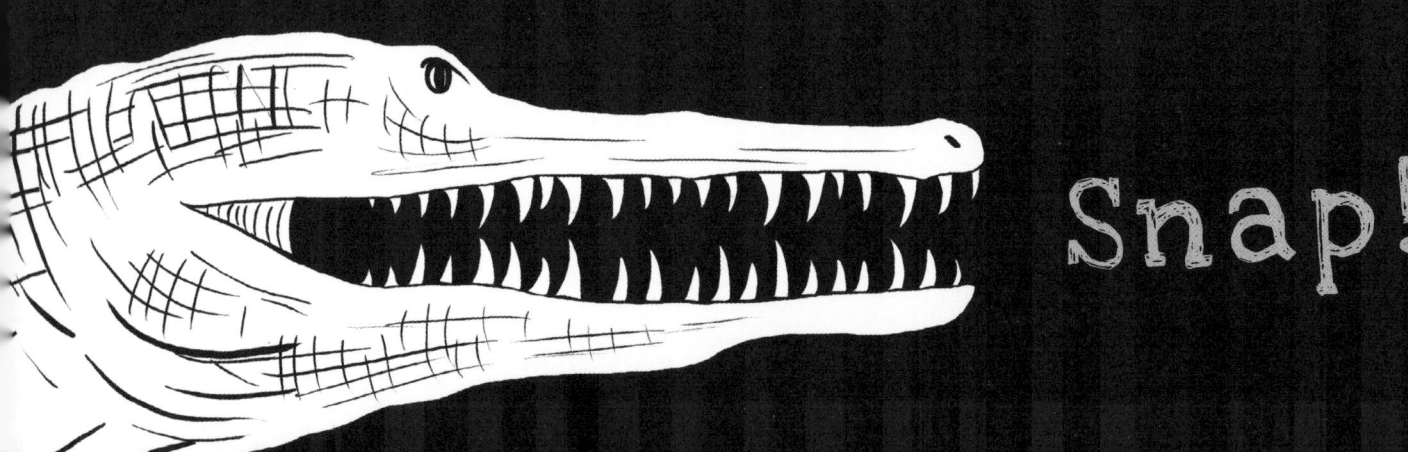

Snap!

Meat-eating dinosaurs are fierce hunters.

Tyrannosaurus rex is armed with a big bite! It uses its sharp eyesight and sense of smell to spot prey.

What is it looking at?

It's *Triceratops*.

Even though this dinosaur has bony horns and a strong beak, the tyrannosaur can easily crunch it up!

Roar!

There are bony plates and spikes all over these *Ankylosauruses*. They will protect them if a meat-eating dinosaur attacks.

What is on the end of this one's swishing tail?

A huge, hard, bony club is at the end of its tail. In a fight, the *Ankylosaurus* swings this weapon at the enemy!

Swish!

This hungry *Baryonyx* has a crocodile-like mouth filled with pointed teeth. It is crouched over the water, watching Something.

Can you see what it's looking at?

Fish!

The dinosaur uses the large claw
on its thumb to hook fish out of the
water, like bears do today.

Swipe!

Today there are no dinosaurs left on Earth. Some scientists think they became extinct because one day, a burning hot meteorite crashed into Earth from space.

Can you guess what happened next?

A dust cloud filled the sky
and blocked the sunlight!

Plants died and the
world became colder. There
was not enough food for
the dinosaurs to eat and
they died out.

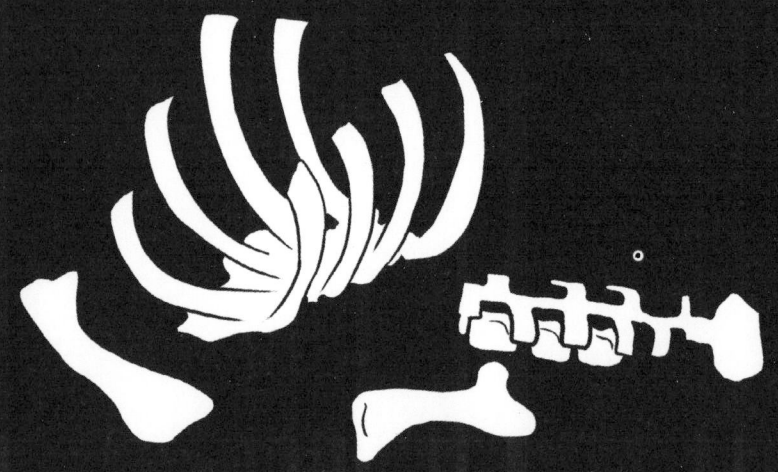
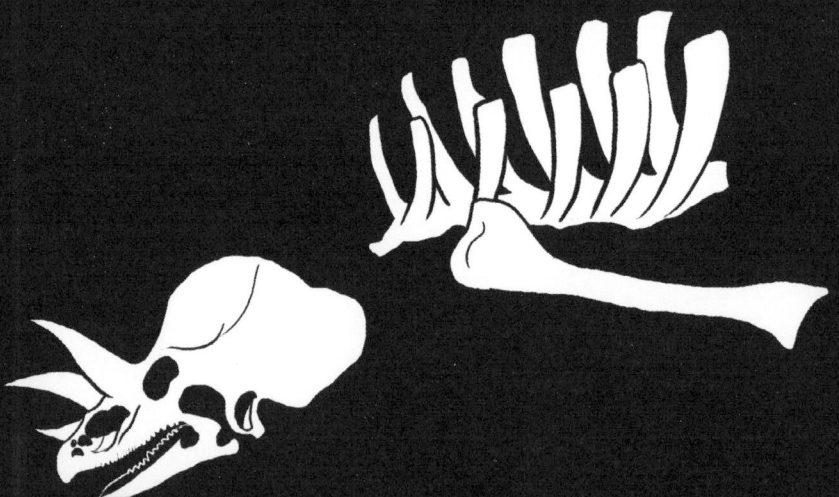

Dinosaurs have been extinct for millions of years, but we know they lived because of the fossils scientists find.

What is buried here?

It's the fossil of a *Stegosaurus*!

Fossils are the bones or other hard parts of something that was alive, which turn into rock after it dies.

If the dinosaurs died out, how are these *Triceratops* still alive?

They're not real!

Museum scientists study fossils to learn all about the dinosaurs, and they recreate dinosaurs and their world so that we can see it, too!

Many smaller animals survived the disaster that ended the age of the dinosaurs. Insects, crocodiles, frogs, fish and mammals are still alive today. And so is a group of small, feathered dinosaur descendants—birds!

There's more...

Studying fossils tells scientists about the dinosaurs that once lived on Earth. Here are some of the awesome discoveries they have made.

Coelophysis had hollow bones. This meant it was light, so it could run quickly to escape from bigger dinosaurs that wanted to catch it.

Pterosaurs were flying reptiles. They soared through the sky on bat-like wings. Some were as small as a sparrow, others as big as a small plane.

Giraffatitan was one of the biggest dinosaurs—almost as tall as three double-decker buses balanced on top of each other!

Parasaurolophus was strange looking! Its mouth was shaped like a duck's beak and filled with hundreds of teeth for grinding up pine needles and other plants it ate.

Tyrannosaurus rex had 60 long, strong, pointed teeth—if any of them wore out, new ones grew! There's a possibility that these dinosaurs were covered in feather-like bristles, too!

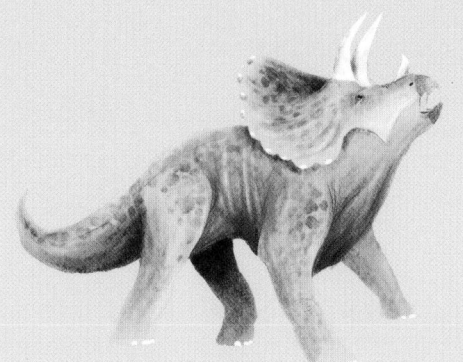

Triceratops weighed as much as two elephants and probably charged its enemies like a modern rhino does. Its long horns were good weapons when a *Tyrannosaurus rex* attacked.

Archaeopteryx was about the size of a crow, with feathers and wings like a modern bird. Scientists are still carrying out tests to find out if it was the first *true* bird.

Deinosuchus was a fearsome giant whose name means "terrible crocodile." It grew longer than 32 feet; its head alone would have been about the same size as a grown man.

First American Edition 2018
Kane Miller, A Division of EDC Publishing

Copyright © 2018 Quarto Publishing plc

For information contact:
Kane Miller, A Division of EDC Publishing
PO Box 470663
Tulsa, OK 74147-0663
www.kanemiller.com
www.edcpub.com
www.usbornebooksandmore.com

Library of Congress Control Number: 2017916537

Printed in China

ISBN: 978-1-61067-717-2

1 2 3 4 5 6 7 8 9 10

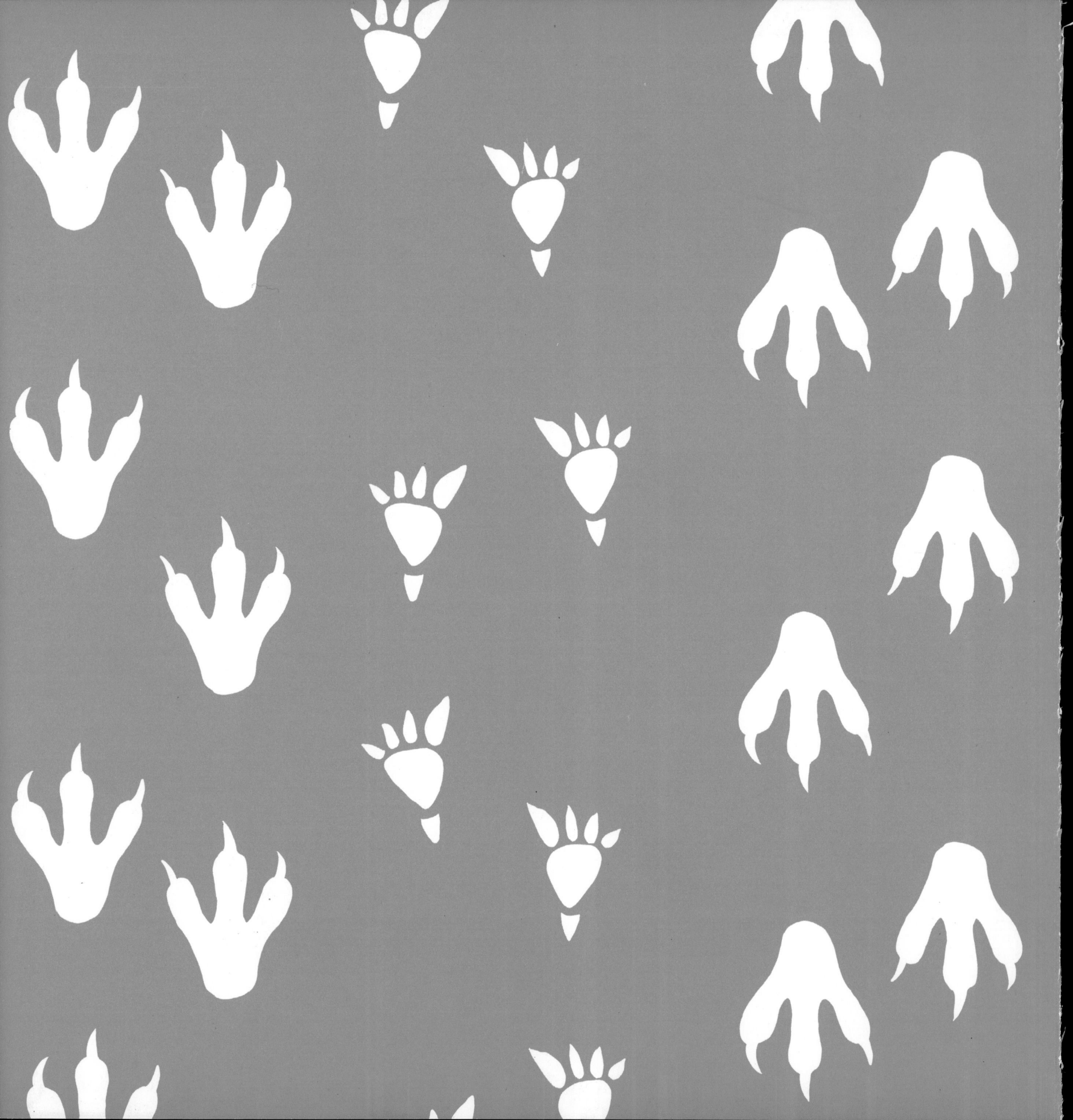